Sept. 2006

Für meine liebe Brunni
und Dich von

Euer Helga

Written by Bjørn Moholdt

Norway

Atmosphere and impressions

Kjerringøy	p.	1
Details from Heddal stave church	p.	3
Bergen	p.	4
The Geiranger Fjord	p.	4-5

Publisher
Incorporate Holding as
Waldemar Thranesgt 77
0175 Oslo

Telephone +47 22 36 06 70
Fax +47 85 03 41 61
E-mail mail@incorporate.no

Text: Bjørn Moholdt, Norway
Picture Editor: Bård Løken, Norway
Translation: ComText as, Norway

Design: Filius Design as,Kristin Stephansen-Smith, Norway
Prepress: Capella Media as, Norway
Printed by Nørhaven A/S, Denmark

Contents

Introduction — p. 9

The history of Norway — p. 15

The Royal Family — p. 22

Urban Life — p. 25
Oslo — p. 25
Lillehammer — p. 29
Tønsberg — p. 30
Drammen — p. 30
Fredrikstad — p. 30
Halden — p. 31
Kongsberg — p. 31
Stavanger — p. 33
Bergen — p. 35
Ålesund — p. 38
Røros — p. 41
Trondheim — p. 43
Tromsø — p. 45
Karasjok — p. 47

The landscape — p. 51
The tundra — p. 51
The fjords — p. 55
Lofoten — p. 62

Diversity — p. 67
An adventure — p. 103

Norwegian trolls and folktales — p. 106

The ten most popular attractions — p. 108

The author's favourites — p. 108

Map — p. 109

About the author — p. 110

About us — p. 110

Captions Norway

L = Left-hand side

R = Right-hand side

J = Joint text

Introduction

"All journeys are but a detour on the way home", I was once told and, during my many years of travel, these words of wisdom have increasingly rung true. Although my work has taken me around the world many times, I am filled with the same sense of gratitude each time I return to Norway.
So what makes this rocky wilderness so alluring, so close as it is to the North Pole and bordering on some of the most inhospitable regions on earth at the very edge of civilisation?

To that I would reply that it is the contrasts - the extremes of coast and interior, fjords and mountains, summer and winter, jagged peaks and endless plateaux.
It goes without saying that nature's overwhelming presence has also shaped the people who have inhabi-

ted this region for some 12,000 years, ever since the first hunters ventured across the Norwegian Trench in search of food.
When the ice receded in the fjords and up in the mountains, it gave way to a coastline and sea that was richly stocked with wild game. Lush green grass grew in the fertile plains that nestled at the heart of the fjords, and on higher ground reindeer

and ptarmigan made their homes between barren mountain ridges. For centuries and right up to the present day, people have come and settled here. The land has provided them with everything they need to survive. Whilst catastrophic famines lay waste to vast swathes of land on the continent, people rarely if ever suffered the same fate here.
The lie of the land made sure of

9

that. Unlike the feudal kingdoms further south, the Norwegians were relatively free to harvest the riches of the sea and the fjords. Life was tough - a meagre existence without compromise, but a sense of local solidarity prospered in the small communities that emerged along the coast and in the valleys and remains a characteristic of this nation to this very day.

Long before the age of aeroplanes, cars, trains and IT, people were separated by topography - fishermen from farmers, farmers from towns-people. The people reflected the lushness and wildness of the land-scape, differences that are still evident today and combine to form a rather unruly nation of which many a politi-cian despairs.

However it is their very determination

that makes Norwegians unique. Urban life is in the process of supp-ressing these idiosyncrasies, which are not so much national traits as local ones and which are extremely diverse. It is tempting to compare Norway's unification by the Viking king Harald Hårfagre at the end of the 800s with the Soviet Union's unnatural federation following the Russian revolution. Norway's formerly autonomous, small kingdoms natu-rally found it difficult to defer to one ruler, and right up to the present day there are many who would argue that Norway continues to be gover-ned by the "chieftains" amongst the fishermen and farmers rather than the politicians.

To a certain extent this is probably true, although Norway has embraced modern times too. We remain a

nation of individualists, with all the advantages and disadvantages this entails, but we are pragmatic enough to realise that it is also important that we interact with the rest of the world as it plays an increasing role in our everyday lives.
This balancing act is something that visitors will find fascinating. The fact that we are to ourselves sufficient, as our world-renowned playwright Henrik Ibsen so eloquently put it, certainly corresponds with my image of Norwegians, and is reflected in all aspects of our lives, from art and culture to industry and tourism.
This self-assurance is not, as some would say, a negative characteristic, but the result of a process lasting ten thousand years, and a force we have not yet managed to tame.

So join us on a fascinating journey through a landscape that promises to be different to anything else you have ever experienced.

Bjørn Moholdt

L: Norway's history is omnipresent, in pageants (Stiklestad), in stone (rocks carvings in Alta) and in architecture (Lom stave church).

R: From the Viking Ship Museum, Bygdøy

The history of Norway

A long, long time ago

Discoveries in the often unproductive Norwegian soil show that the first inhabitants in Norway arrived in the country some 12,000 years ago, during the last Ice Age. The colossal glaciers subsided to reveal fjords teeming with fish, seals and whales, and at the heart of the fjords an abundance of game.

Strangely enough the first definite traces of people in Norway are to be found in the very north of the country, not far from the North Cape. At Sarnes on the island of Magerøya, trappers have left behind arrowheads and knives made of stone, as well as scrapers that were used to clean hides.
However, all the signs suggest that the hunters on the coast of Finnmark came from the south and were des-

cendants of trappers who settled along the south coast. They probably found their way to Norway across the ice during the winter, or arrived in small leather boats during the summer.

Discoveries of even earlier remnants of bones from reindeer, seals, whales and different species of fish suggest that winter hunters came from the North Sea lands south of the Norwegian Trench, a continuous continent extending from modern-day Scotland across to Denmark and Skåne. Finds from the oldest settlement in Southern Norway, at Tranhaug on the northern tip of Rennesøy in Rogaland, suggest that from around the year 9000 B.C. the area was occupied at different times by reindeer hunters, polar-bear hunters and fishermen.

At that time, Norway was an inhospitable region, far colder than a thousand years earlier. The groups of hunters that operated here were extremely dispersed and were probably descendants of specialist big-game hunters. Around 8000 B.C. the whole of Europe suddenly became considerably warmer. The glaciers subsided and the reindeer - the most important animal for barter for the trappers - disappeared into the mountains. Quickly followed by the hunters.

The strongest testimony to the first hunters to settle in Norway is found in rock carvings. Images of animals and people were hammered, chiselled, carved or coloured into the bare rock-face. Over a thousand sites with Stone and Bronze Age rock carvings throughout Norway depict a vibrant culture, in which the animals for barter were all-important.

The relatively good hunting and fishing conditions in Northern Europe meant that the first hunter farmer – or Stone Age farmer – did not emerge until around 2000 B.C. However, agricultural developments and the establishment of permanent settle-

The vessels were sophisticated and capable of travelling fast and far. They were also important instruments in the growing rivalry between the small kingdoms that emerged in the 800s.

The expansion of the Roman Empire had led to greater contact with the outside world, after several hundred years of virtual isolation. The runes -

ments meant that the population was able to multiply.

The arrival of the Vikings

With the sea as an important transport artery, the Norwegians soon became accomplished sailors, constructing boats using a technique that remains a technological mystery to this day.

the 24-character written language particular to Scandinavia that emerged around 200 A.D. - indicate strong influences from Greek and Roman cultures.

The bloody clashes between the many chieftains in Norway, combined with a general wanderlust, led to the Viking expeditions that began towards the end of the 700s and lasted just over

200 years. In around 890 Norway was united by Harald Hårfagre, who became the country's first king. At around the same time, Iceland was colonised and Ireland subjected to Norwegian rule.

A particular characteristic of the Vikings was their ability to easily assimilate with their surroundings. This ability to merge into the local communities was

J: Håkonshallen in Bergen (from left), details from Urnes stave church, traditional folk dancing at the Norwegian Museum of Cultural History.

quite unique. For example William the Conqueror, the archetypal Norman –chieftain, was of Viking blood. This key figure in British history was a descendant of the famous Viking chieftain Rollo, who had conquered Normandy a hundred years previously.

Norwegians have continued to display a special ability to adapt in more recent times. In the mid-1800s and the early 1900s, some one million of us emigrated in two large waves to the promised land - America, where we played a part in helping to build the modern USA.

An Irish source dating from 874 refers to King Ivar in Dublin as king of all Norwegians in Ireland and Great Britain. This is the first time in history that the word "nordmenn" - the people of the north - is mentioned.

The Vikings carried out raids across the whole of Europe, beginning in the British Isles and gradually making their way down to the Mediterranean, plundering for goods and gold. They raided Paris, Seville and Lisbon, and

reached as far west as North America 500 years before Christopher Columbus began the search for a new route to India.

The many Viking expeditions brought wealth to Norway in the form of goods and gold, but cultural impulses together with the importation of new vegetables and farming methods also contributed to a vastly improved way of life for most Norwegians.

As a result of the many blood feuds, and knowledge of the Germanic legal system wergeld, the small communities also developed systems of government in the form of regional parliaments - or ting - where laws were drawn up and disputes settled.

J: Constitution Day celebrations in front of the Palace (from left), the speaker's platform at the Storting (Norwegian parliament) and café life in the capital.

Top R. Fjørtoft stave church.

With the establishment of a centralised monarch, conflicts arose that were to leave their mark on the country. The constant rivalry between Viking chieftains and the royal house culminated in the historic battle of Stiklestad in the year 1030, at which Olav (the Holy) Haraldsson, later canonised as St. Olav, was killed

Throughout these years, the Vikings continued with their raids, albeit on a smaller scale, but all this ended after the epic battle at Stamford Bridge, where the Norwegian king Harald Hardråde's attempt to conquer England ended in vain.

Light at the end of the tunnel
Following a new period of civil wars and major internal divisions, Norway as a nation was strengthened at every level, thanks in large part to strong monarchs such as King Sverre and Magnus Lagabøter.

Then, in 1319, the country acquired a common monarch with Sweden, signifying the beginning of the end for Norway as an independent nation. Moreover, a few years later the country was invaded by a danger that no military power could withstand: the Black Death.

The plague ravaged the whole of Europe, transmitted by fleas borne by rats. It was brought to Norway by an English merchant ship in 1349. The Black Death, which claimed the lives of more than a third of the population, wiped out entire communities and with it most of the social structure. Added to this, an already greatly weakened nation was united with Sweden and

laws and a foreign written language.

On May 17 1814, Norway took its first tentative steps out of the darkness by declaring its independence from Sweden, which had taken over the country as part of the peace treaty in Kiel following the Napoleonic wars. A short war ensued, until Norway agreed to a union with Sweden.

J: Hardanger fiddle.

Nesseby church, Varanger Fjord, Finnmark.

Part of Oslo City Hall and the Oseberg ship on Bygdøy peninsula.

Denmark under Danish rule by the Union of Kalmar.

Norway's position was continuously undermined, and the country gradually slid into what historians refer to as "the 400-year night". In the mid-1500s the once proud Viking people of the north were a mere shadow of their former selves, and Norway no more than a Danish province, subject to foreign

During the 90 years of Swedish domination that followed, there were dramatic developments in a number of areas, leading to the dissolution of the union in 1905 and to Norwegian independence. Norway as a nation developed role models and "flag bearers" who to this day are symbols of this nascent nation.
In cultural terms at least, the country flourished. The composer Edvard Grieg,

inspired by Norwegian folk music, became a household name across the world. As did the expressionist painter Edvard Munch, the playwright Henrik Ibsen and the author and Nobel Prize winner Knut Hamsun. They all experienced their most creative periods at the end of the 1800s and in the early 1900s, and were deeply rooted in Norwegian culture and mythology. At the same time, the country was undergoing a political awakening, largely led by the eminent politician Johan Sverdrup, who was at the forefront of the development of the Norwegian parliament, the Storting, and full independence from the Swedish Crown.

During these years, heroes also emerged in other areas, heroes who were to define the nation and still symbolise the country. The polar explorer Roald Amundsen, the first man to reach the South Pole, and Fridtjof Nansen, were international personalities who put Norway firmly on the world map.

In later years, the author and scientist Thor Heyerdahl has followed in Amundsen's and Nansen's footsteps as a geopolitical role model.

Around a hundred years earlier - in the mid-1800s - the industrial revolution had begun in Norway and, on a seemingly shaky basis, commerce and industry gra-

level as the spring of 1940. Despite the fact that the merchant fleet, which had contributed greatly to the Allies' war efforts, had been halved, it did not take long for this shipping nation to find its feet again. In the 1950s, basic goods were still being rationed in society, although the reconstruction period began to produce results. Norway was on its way... With the discovery of oil in the same areas across which the first

dually developed. The country excelled within maritime activities in particular, although cheap hydroelectric power also played an important role in its industrialisation.

From rags to riches

On 9 April 1940 Germany contravened Norwegian neutrality by invading the country. It took two months to quash the final vestiges of opposition. King Haakon VII and his government were able to escape to England with Norway's gold bullion, and a five-year long occupation ensued.

After the Second World War, developments accelerated. Only three years after the war ended, the country's gross domestic product had reached the same

Norwegians had travelled some 12,000 years previously, the circle was completed. In just 50 years Norway had transformed itself from one of Europe's poorest nations to one of the world's richest and was again somewhere which held out the promise of the good life.

The Royal Family

The Norwegian Royal Family still plays an important role in this country, despite its declining significance over the years. The young royals, represented here by Crown Princess Mette-Marit and Crown Prince Haakon (left) and Princess Märtha Louise and her husband Ari Behn (below), are popular with the general public, as are the King and Queen (bottom centre).

The Royal Palace

The royal palace, which was built between 1825 and 1848, is located at the far end of the capital's main thoroughfare, Karl Johan. The building was recently renovated at great expense and is today a magnificent example of superb architectural interior design.

L: Holmenkollbakken, the world's best-known ski jump.

R: A winter's evening in Oslo's main thoroughfare, Karl Johan.

Urban life

Oslo

Oslo is Scandinavia's oldest capital. The name is derived from the Old Norse words às, meaning god, and lo, meaning meadow. The town was probably established in around 995 A.D., although the well-known chronicler and historian Snorre Sturlason described Harald Hardråde as its founder in around 1048.

Although a while later Harald's son Olav Kyrre made Oslo the cathedral city, it did not become the home of the monarch until the 1300s, when King Håkon V relocated to Oslo from Bergen and built Akershus fortress. After a period of strong growth, the Black Death virtually decimated the

town. It was the Danish king Christian IV, following a rampant town fire in 1624, who decided to move the town to its present location under the protection of Akershus fortress, at the same time modestly renaming it Christiania.

Christiania, as the town was known right up to 1925, experienced a resurgence that continues to this day. However, it was largely the industrial revolution at the end of the 19th century that turned Oslo into the country's financial and political centre.

As a visitor, it is worth taking in the many superb museums.

Vikingeskipmuseet (The Viking Ship Museum) is magnificent and provides a wonderful introduction to Norwegian history seen from the country's most glorious historical period.
Skimuseet (The Ski Museum) in Holmenkollen is a reminder of Norway's close links with nature and sports, and the importance of the country's heroes to the formation of our national identity.
Munchmuseet (The Munch Museum) displays several of the key works of Norway's best-known artist Edvard Munch. And not to be missed is the truly impressive and monumental Vigelandsparken sculpture park.

25

J: Highlights from (from left)
Holmenkollen, the Storting and Aker Brygge.

Only a very few people outside Norway are familiar with the sculptor Gustav Vigeland, however his name will most certainly be etched in the minds of most people after a visit to the park that bears his name. Vigeland's work to embellish the park area located slightly to the northwest of Oslo town centre took several years to complete, but is a masterpiece that remains unrivalled in the world.

Although Oslo has in recent years acquired a reputation for being a fiery, self-confident and cosmopolitan capital, boasting exquisite restaurants and a huge variety of cultural attractions and nightlife, the town is most closely associated with its proximity to nature. Not far from the town centre you can ski or walk by yourself in vast woodlands. You can swim in the many small lakes or off the numerous beaches on the edge of the Oslofjord. The different districts also offer beautiful parks and outdoor cafes that are buzzing all through the summer. All in all, you would search hard to find its equal.

The Kon-Tiki Museum in Oslo
The balsawood raft Kon-Tiki was built as a copy of a prehistoric South American vessel. Constructed of nine balsa logs collected from Equador, a crew of six men sailed the raft from Callao in Peru on 28th April 1947 and landed on the island of Raroia in Polynesia 101 days later. This successful 4300-mile voyage proved that the islands in Polynesia were within the range of this type of prehistoric South American vessel.

Hadeland Glassworks - Norway's oldest manufacturing Company

Hadeland Glassworks, founded in 1762 by the Danish King Christian IV, stands at the southern end of the beautiful Randsfjord. As there were no professional glassblowers in Norway at that time, they were recruited from Germany and later from Bohemia and England. Even today there are workers at the factory who can trace their roots back to those first glassblowers.

To begin with, production centred on bottles, flasks and chemist's phials, however from 1852 it shifted towards fine glasswork and everything from wine glasses to bowls, plates and vases. Hadeland Glassworks is also a major player in the production of decorative glass.

Until 1814 the Norwegian glassworks were owned by the Dano-Norwegian state under the King and a few of his closest men, however post-Eidsvoll, all Danish property in Norway was reclaimed by the new Norwegian state, and in 1824 the glassworks were privatised.

To visit Norway's oldest manufacturing company is to embark on a journey through history marked by the highest standards of taste and good design. Hadeland Glassworks has preserved and developed the art of glassmaking and given it a unique position in Norwegian cultural history. No other manufacturer in Norway has such a long tradition of handcraft. Here visitors may witness some of Europe's finest glassblowers practising their craft, then visit Norway's only museum devoted to glassmaking. Hadeland Glassworks can offer a wide range of attractions – the tin foundry, candle foundry, Christmas House, Hunny House, bakery and restaurant, as well as a factory shop and an art gallery where, every summer, artists from around the world exhibit their works.

Lillehammer

Lillehammer is located at the northern end of Norway's largest lake, by the entrance to the Gudbrandsdalen valley – quintessential, rural Norway.

Located at the geographical heartland of Southern Norway, Lillehammer became famed the world over after hosting the Winter Olympic Games in 1994. In conjunction with this, billions of kroner were invested in infrastructure and sports facilities, giving the town and the surrounding area a much needed boost.

The Lillehammer region is not only a superb starting point for winter activities but, in the wake of the Olympics, has also become a popular area for holiday homes. The opportunities for various activities such as downhill skiing, cross-country skiing, fishing, cycling, mountain walks and canoeing are attracting more and more people, and not only from Norway.

Top left: Slottsfjellet in Tønsberg, view over Drammen.

J: Several of the smaller towns around the Oslofjord bear influence to their proximity to Europe and the wars that have raged over the centuries. Both the Old Town in Fredrikstad (left) and Fredriksten Fortress in Halden are beautiful monuments to a bygone age.

R: The crowns carved into Hovet in Kongsberg are reminders of the Norwegian kings who visited the old mining town.

Tønsberg, Fredrikstad, Halden, Drammen and Kongsberg

J: For many Norwegians, summers are synonymous with southern Norway, where they migrate to in droves at this time of year. The zoo (bottom left), Otterdalsparken (top) in Kristiansand and Pollen in the centre of Arendal are particular favourites.

J: Stavanger's old timber houses are kept in pristine condition.

Stavanger

Stavanger has always been somewhat overshadowed by Bergen, however its survival instincts are enviable.

Communities of all sizes along the Norwegian coast have always relied upon the supply of fish in the sea. The same is true of Stavanger, which built up much of its economy on the herring fisheries. However, unlike most others, Stavanger knew where to turn when the fish stocks dwindled and its salvation came in the form of shipbuilding. In more recent years, oil has rescued this lively town and, with the discovery of oil on the Continental shelf and the crowning of Stavanger as the oil capital of Norway, the really serious money began to pour in.

It also has a nightlife that can compete with what you would expect to find in far larger towns..

The most fascinating aspect of Stavanger is nevertheless not the town itself, but the surrounding countryside, in particular the fjords. The spectacular Lysefjorden is one of nature's wonders, which you should not miss as you make your way along the coast.

J: Many people associate Bergen with its myriad alleyways, or with Fantoft stave church (top left). But possibly the most impressive and defining feature of the capital of the fjords are the old "German wharves" that nestle alongside the harbour, which were once the base of the Hanseatic League who ruled the town at the time.

Bergen

According to one of the country's foremost writers, the route to Norway is via the fjords. And "the capital of the fjords" is Bergen. Brimming with self-confidence, it is more reminiscent of an autonomous Italian Renaissance town.

This is attributable to the town's deep-seated traditions as a commercial town. Bergen has always had its sights set on the outside world. The Hanseatic League's presence in the town, which lasted several hundreds of years, is one of the major reasons for this.

Its old timber houses that nestle alongside the harbour and its surrounding mountains are a magnificent sight to behold. Founded by King Olav Kyrre in 1070, Bergen was the largest and most important town in Norway in the Middle Ages, and the most populous right up to the 1800s.

In the 13th century, the west country capital became an important member of the Hanseatic League, and German influence on its trade lasted several hundred years.

The timber houses that line Bryggen wharf where the German merchants were based run off Torget, a busy, outdoor fish market which is well worth a visit. People from Bergen who have been away often feel that they are not really home again until

they have popped into Torget and Torgalmenningen immediately above it.

The architecture and surrounding countryside are strikingly beautiful, however it is also worth taking in several of Bergen's museums. Norges Fiskerimuseum (the Norwegian Fisheries Museum) in particular provides a vivid insight into the unique Norwegian coastal culture on which Bergen depended to a large extent.

Fantoft stave church is a fascinating example of original, Norwegian church architecture in the Middle Ages and you should also aim to see the composer Edvard Grieg's home Troldhaugen on the outskirts of the town.

J: Bergen is one of Norway's most picturesque towns. Highlights from Bryggen (far left), from Fløien towards Vägen (top), the fish market (left) and Troldhaugen (above), the former home of Norway's most famous composer Edvard Grieg.

P. 38 39: Ålesund

Røros

J: Røros is listed as a UNESCO World Heritage Site, and is caught in a time warp from the time when the copper mines founded the town over 300 years ago.
Dominating the town's profile are the vast slag heaps that tower over the old, mean miners' cottages beneath them (bottom left).

J: Nidaros Cathedral (left and top right), a sacred national treasure, dates from around 1070 and was completed in around 1320. The town bridge (below right) is one of many distinctive bridges over the Nidelva River.

Trondheim

Up until the 16th century Trondheim was known as Nidaros, and was a political power base in the country. Nidaros Cathedral, one of Scandinavia's most impressive medieval buildings, was known throughout the world as an important destination for pilgrims.

Following a huge fire in 1681, the centre of Trondheim was entirely rebuilt, according to a plan that included wide avenues drawn up by Caspar de Cicignon, a military engineer from Luxembourg. It is to him that the town largely owes its air of openness, tranquillity and elegance, complemented by pleasant, patient and sympathetic locals.
Trondheim is the country's "agricultural capital", due to the, by Norwegian standards, extensive fertile countryside and the many farms that surround the town.
Many of the buildings from the town's economic heyday at the end of the 19th century remain intact, and give Trondheim its unique charm.

J: One of the most distinctive buildings in Tromsø is the Arctic Ocean Cathedral (bottom left and right). The Polaria research and administration centre (far left) and the bust of the explorer Roald Amundsen (left) are testament to the town's past and present importance for Norway's tradition of polar expeditions.

Tromsø

Tromsø is often referred to as the Paris of the North not, as many believe, as a result of today's varied nightlife and music but due to its trendsetting inhabitants in the 19th century who invested a lot of energy in importing the latest fashions from the French capital.

This did not escape the attention of the many visitors to the town, and Tromsø acquired its reputation for being an exciting and diverse town which it retains today.

Tromsø was and continues to be a commercially important town in the north, often referred to as the capital of Northern Norway. The town flourished in the 1800s when polar bear, reindeer and seal trapping took off in a big way.

Tromsø also became famed as the starting point for several major polar expeditions, not least the one that ended in the death of the country's best-known adventurer Roald Amundsen's in the icy wastes surrounding the North Pole in 1928.

J: The Sami people have reclaimed their pride and carry their flags and wear their national dress – as illustrated by Roger Hætta in Kautokeino (top left) – with pride.

Karasjok

The Sami's capital lies in a valley on Finnmarksvidda, and is a power base for a culture that is being kept very much alive despite fierce opposition in the 1900s. These days visitors will encounter a proud race, with a unique past.

Karasjok is home to this ancient people's parliament - Sametinget - which was set up when the revitalisation of the Sami culture took off in earnest in the early 1980s.
Also worth visiting in Karasjok is the museum of Sami collections, De Samiske Samlinger, and the Samelandssenteret centre, which provides a vivid portrayal of the development of the Sami culture on the Nordkalotten.

Birch forest

The Northern Lights (Aurora Borealis)

J: Wild reindeer in the Norwegian mountains,
where cotton grass (right) is a cherished feature.

The landscape

The tundra

A few years ago, I was suddenly awoken early one morning by someone lying very close to me shivering. I had volunteered to follow the Sami family Somby's annual spring migration with the reindeer herd from Finnmarksvidda out to the coast.

It had been 20 degrees Celsius below zero the day before and quiet on the tundra but according to Nils, the head of the family, the skies heralded bad weather. He was right, and the following day, as we were set-

ting up camp by the coast, a south-westerly storm swept across the countryside making all movement outside our tent virtually impossible.

But Nils was more concerned about his animals, and late that evening he set out in the darkness, ignoring the blizzard, to check that the reindeer were comfortable. I eventually fell asleep and awoke a good while later to find that he had lain down next to me for warmth. For several hours, he had battled astride his snow scooter through the storm, finally seeking shelter under cover of an animal skin blanket in the vicinity of the herd. He dug himself out again once daylight made it a little easier to return to the camp.

I have no idea how he found his

Some things just cannot be explained. But the old man had made this journey many times before, and had spent an entire lifetime living in tune with a landscape that for several hundred years has provided his family with the very basis for life. The movement of the reindeer is no longer a virtue of necessity for the Sami, but the tradition has overcome financial incentives. Nils became

way there and back or how he managed to navigate in the darkness between dwarf birches and moraine, up through steep escarpments and down deep gullies. Nils simply smiled his inscrutable smile when I asked, and instead busied himself preparing the casserole of reindeer meat that was always bubbling away on our stove in the middle of the tent.

restless if the reindeer did not begin moving towards the coast before the female reindeer began calving. Ancient instincts are not so easily banished.

The Norwegian tundra is magnificent, and visitors are able to join the Sami on the annual spring migration. Despite the fact that it no longer has any social or financial significance,

Reindeer herding in minus 40 degrees Celsius is no easy job, even for a people who have been doing this for centuries.

many Sami reindeer herders do it simply for the sake of tradition. The journey is not only a unique way in which to experience the magnificent tundra landscape, but a wonderful opportunity to get to know one of Europe's few remaining ancient peoples.

The tundra in Finnmark in the very north of Norway is perhaps, on first impression, not so very different to

Besseggen in Jotunheimen is well known from Norwegian folklore, literature and drama.

Hardangervidda, which is home to Europe's last wild reindeer stock. However, where the tundra in the south is wilder and more barren, in Finnmark it is more fertile, with river valleys full of tall grass that provides shelter for both people and animals.

If you are lucky enough on Hardangervidda, Europe's largest mountain plateau, you may even

spot the wild reindeer. However, it is a shy animal that has learnt from experience to keep its distance from humans. After all, ever since the ice melted people have hunted this fascinating animal here, an animal which has adapted to life on a bare minimum.

Today, wild reindeer hunting is purely recreational and the region it has to roam in is constantly shrinking.

The fjords

To the west, Hardangervidda plunges deep into a picturesque fjord landscape, namely Hardangerfjorden, which empties into a spectacular archipelago of different sized islands south of Bergen.
It is no wonder that so many people associate Norway with its fjords. Our coastline is heavily indented by large and small fjord arms, an ongoing nightmare for road authorities and railway enthusiasts, but an unparalleled sight nevertheless.

J: The Norwegian fjords can take your breath away, particularly when viewed from the top of Pulpit Rock in Lysefjorden. Nærøyfjorden (left), a side fjord of Norway's longest fjord, Sognefjorden, is described as the world's narrowest fjord arm.

Particularly spectacular is the Sognefjorden, 180 kilometres deep, with inlets you would be foolish to miss. In order to gain a certain understanding of how the enormous fjords came into being, you should pause in Fjærland, where you will find Norsk Bremuseum (The Norwegian Glacier Museum), depicting how the fjord landscape was created:

During the Ice Age some three million years ago, the whole of Scandinavia was covered by ice. Slowly but surely the ice moved out towards the sea, and on its journey dug out the existing mountain valleys which then became filled with seawater. The pressure from the vast quantities of ice inland pressed the fjords below the level of the bottom of the sea. At its deepest point,

Sognefjorden, for example, is 1308 metres deep, ten times deeper than most places in the Norwegian Sea.

The Gulf Stream from the west provided life-giving, temperate water from the Caribbean, which kept the fjords free of ice and guaranteed summers inside the deep fjords that are comparable to what you would expect to find far further south in

J: View of Aurlandsfjorden, which carves its way southwards from Sognefjorden.

Europe. It can get warm and hot, something that has also enabled extensive fruit farming to flourish in several of the fjords.

You can follow the fjord landscape all the way along the Norwegian coast, via Vestfjorden at the heart of Lofoten in the far north to the broad Porsangerfjorden, and out to Varangerfjorden in the east, which opens out towards the abundantly stocked fishing banks in the Barents Sea.

The village of Fjærland, which nestles inside the narrow and precipitous Fjærlandsfjorden, was for a long time caught in a time warp, due to its location inside a narrow side fjord of Sognefjorden - isolated from the rest of the

57

Today the many paths that led up to the mountain summer farms and summer pastures for the cows have been taken over by tourists, who use them to gain access to the magnificent mountain range that surrounds Fjærland.

Places like Fjærland are few and far between in Fjord Norway, but there are several that resemble it. Prosperity brought more and better roads deeper into the fjords, and today most places are easily accessible by car. You should, however, allow yourself plenty of time because it is easy to fall under the spell of this beautiful countryside, which will make you want to stay.

world. The village did not get a road connection until 1986, and the locals still speak a dialect which even a Norwegian needs a practised ear to understand.
At the same time the village's old, well preserved, timber houses provide an impression of what life must have been like in these west country fjords, at a time when people had to survive on what the soil, the sea and a few cows could provide.

J: The fjord landscape is varied and beautiful and Geirangerfjorden (right) is particularly spectacular.

J: There is certainly no shortage of water in
Norway, whether in waterfalls, such as in
Flåmsdalen (left), by Sørfjorden in
Hardangerfjorden (far left) or tranquil waters such
as in Isfjorden in Romsdal (above).

Lofoten

Of Norway's many natural treasures, Lofoten is perhaps the greatest.
Arriving from the south by boat, you are met by a breath-taking spectacle. Lofotveggen - the archipelago's jagged, continuous mountain formation - rises on the horizon like a monument over this island kingdom.

In this ocean region, generations of people have harvested spawning cod, which played a major role in the establishment of Bergen as a key financial centre in Norway. Most of the fish was sent southwards, where the serious money was.

J: Fishing is the very lifeblood of Lofoten, and dried fish (right) is an important article for export. Puffins (above) thrive in this dramatic landscape.

Cod was and continues to be a precious commodity for the fishermen, but times have changed. The many fishermen's shacks that previously housed poor, wizened labourers are now charming places in which to stay for the many visitors who come here every year.

Lofoten is still a vibrant community, where fishermen carry out their everyday tasks side by side with the visitors. The Gulf Stream ensures dry and relatively mild winters and, the weather gods permitting, this means that the fish can be dried and stored indefinitely.

Already in the Viking Period, the Norsemen took dried fish with them in their

longships when they set out on expeditions, and it was the distinctive drying racks that caught visitors' attention when they first came.

The Italian seafarer Pietro Querini, who, together with his crew, was shipwrecked on Røst at the outermost point of Lofoten in the 1400s, gives a detailed description of this in his careful records from his involuntary stay of several months there. Querini was fascinated by the harmony in which the people here lived, in a seamless symbiosis with the wild countryside. "The first glimpse of paradise", he wrote in a detailed and fascinating report of the journey, and two of the crew elaborated on his captivation:

"The people here are extremely friendly and helpful towards each other, eager to accommodate each other, more out of love than in the hope of any favour or return."

A glimpse into the heart and soul of the people of Northern Norway, I would say, in a region where the value of solidarity is understood. Without each other we are small, something that makes the people in this beautiful but often inhospitable landscape in Northern Norway unpretentious and welcoming.

J: For several hundred years, fishermen have plundered the treasures of the sea, from fishing vessels that have changed radically over the years. The fishermen's shacks remain more or less intact (left) but are now used mostly by visitors.

J: A nation of contrasts – nestling between fjords and mountains, southern Norway (left) and Jotunheimen (above right).

Diversity

In many ways the Norwegian interior contrasts strongly with the coast, where people were more mobile and often received visitors from the outside world.

It is therefore easy to forget the many natural gems to be found in Southern Norway, trapped as they are between the fjords in the west and Sweden in the east, but nevertheless wide enough to make up a substantial part of the Norwegian mainland.

During the summer, large numbers of the Norwegian population migrate to the strip of coast in the far south. In Southern Norway and on both sides of Oslofjorden, you will find beautiful beaches, small island groups and idyllic bays where you can hide yourself away.

Previous pages: J: On the southernmost tip of Norway – as here by Lindesnes lighthouse (left) and Lista (bottom right) – it is almost as if the land has been scrubbed clean by the sea. The close links to the sea are also reflected in the yacht harbour, Kragerø (above right)

As I mentioned in the introduction to this book, Norway is a nation of contrasts, and it is often in this contrast between the sea and the interior that you will find many of the most interesting attractions. The winter season is also greatly underestimated. "There is no such thing as bad weather, only poor clothing", is an expression Norwegians never seem to tire of quoting, but which also reflects our relationship with the elements.

J: Water plays an important part in Norwegian summers.

J: More and more people are discovering
Norway's countless natural gems. The Telemark
Canal (top right) is a magnificent way to discover
the hinterland of eastern Norway. Sommarland in
Bø (above centre) is a favourite destination for
children. Far left, Heddal stave church.

Previous pages: Gaustatoppen

J: Nature is all around, whether in the form of a
hawk owl or a cow moose following you with its
watchful eye, or a thundering waterfall, such as
Dønfossen in Ottadalen (bottom right).

J: The forests in winter are magical.

J: The gathering clouds cast a shadow over Glittertinden in Jotunheimen (above left). In the deep valley below, a peony plant emerges from the heather, and on Buarbreen in Folgefonna the forces of nature are being challenged.

The colour scheme in the mountains changes in tune with the seasons, from brilliant white, like the peaks in Rondane (top right) to the fiery red of Geiranger (left), where you may even be lucky enough to catch a glimpse of the shy ptarmigan.

83

P.84-85: Geirangerfjorden

J: For periods of time, people in Norway lived in cramped conditions and it was common for them to move their livestock to summer dwellings (above) in the mountains. Today, mountain summer dairying, such as at Herdalssetra in Norddal (top left) is mostly for the benefit of tourists.

Pages 88-89:

J: Right up until the middle of the last century, farming was carried out on steep mountain slopes, such as on the mountain farm Blomberg (Bottom left) by Geirangerfjorden (right). Top left, Eidsvatnet in Eidsdal.

Pages 90-91:

J: As you can see from these pictures, building roads in Norway is an expensive undertaking. However, the winding roads will bring you in close contact with the magnificent countryside. Clockwise from left, Flåmsbanen railway line, Knuten in Geiranger, Briksdalen, the Trollstigen road between Åndalsnes and Låtefoss in Odda.

Pages 92 - 93:

Briksdalsbreen glacier, Vøringsfossen waterfall

The Arctic Circle (66° 33' N) is the geographical border with the Arctic regions. The Arctic Circle Centre provides information on culture, history, trade and industry, tourism, attractions and places of interest in Northern Norway. A marker going right through the building indicates the position of the Arctic Circle.

Saltstraumen near Bodø
What is perhaps the world's most powerful tidal current is a tremendous sight, an enormous mass of water which is forced into a strait three kilo-metres long and just 15 metres wide at speeds of up to 20 knots. Fishing here can be thrilling.

Reine, Lofoten (right)

The Alta Igloo Hotel measures 1,600 square metres. The entire exterior and interior is made of snow and ice: the rooms, the beds, even the glasses in the bar!

Hammerfest

J: The North Cape (above) is the destination for over a hundred thousand visitors to Norway each year.

An adventure

The battle against the elements has played a large part in shaping the heart and soul of the Norwegian people, and is one of the reasons why Norwegians are so obsessed with outdoor activities. The magnificent countryside is another obvious reason.

The most eminent Norwegian personalities have also been drawn to nature, particularly the polar regions. In 1911 the adventurer Roald Amundsen battled through icy blizzards in the race to be the first person to reach the South Pole, whilst Fridtjof Nansen attracted attention with his expeditions around the ice of the North Pole.

In the early years following independence from Sweden in 1905, it became important for this nascent and, in a global context, relatively insignificant nation to create a strong national identity. The sporting heroes and adventurers were therefore our strongest ambassadors in the international arena, something they continue to be, though to a lesser extent over the years.

This fact has encouraged ordinary men and women to get out into the countryside, whether on skis, on foot in the mountains or on a vessel in the waters off our long and ragged coastline. Cross-country skiing is our national sport. It embraces all types of people and all ages, and has produced our most important heroes.

J: Norwegians are born with skis on their feet, as documented by The Ski Museum in Oslo (above). However there are many other pursuits to be enjoyed on your own throughout the year, including sea kayaking, as here on Moskenesøy in Lofoten (left).

Glacier walking in Jotunheimen (right) is something anyone can take part in, but usually requires a local guide, as does river rafting (Sjoa above). A quiet walk in the woods is enough for most people and Oslo's Nordmarka has several cabins that welcome visitors arriving by foot or on skis, such as Ullevålseteren (left).

Nordmarka north of Oslo, only a few minutes' drive by car from the centre of the capital, is a cherished destination for thousands of people. As a visitor, this is where you get the strongest sense of Norwegians' yearning for nature.

The age-old urge to travel that began with the Vikings over a thousand years ago is also evident in a number of other areas. No others are as keen hunters as us, or as eager to catch fish in rivers, lakes and in the sea. This is something that even visitors have noticed, and often come here to participate in themselves. The choices are endless.

The opportunities to enjoy the countryside and join in the many activities are countless irrespective of where in the country you choose to

holiday. You can walk across the large glaciers in the southwest, or cycle over the mountains along the old routes between Oslo and Trondheim. In Northern Norway, you can go sea fishing or simply head off in speedboats on the crests of the waves.

In the north, the winter offers dog sled or snow scooter expeditions across Finnmarksvidda

Activities in Norway are not primarily designed with tourists in mind. Most activities are based on the local population's own interests and traditions and therefore have an enchanting cultural aspect.

On your journey through the Norwegian countryside you will not lack any of the equipment required. If there is one thing we are good at it is preparation. Without good planning, preparation and the right clothes, Amundsen would never have reached the South Pole. Seemingly obvious, but nevertheless oh so difficult. But do not despair: you can lean on traditions that date back to the Viking Period.

In other words you are in safe hands.

Norwegian trolls and folktales

For generations, Norwegian children have been fed images of make-believe characters such as trolls, sirens and goblins. The stories and legends have been passed from family to family, from generation to generation.

These days we no longer believe in the existence of these mythical creatures. Nevertheless, the stories are told and retold at bedtime to children and grandchildren all over Norway. They form an important part of Norway's cultural heritage. Stories from other countries may feature creatures that resemble trolls, but there is something particularly Norwegian about trolls. They have very special characteristics that make them Norwegian.

Folktales have played an important role in Norway. Historical, political and cultural developments have all helped to shape the stories and, in turn, these stories provided valuable national symbols when it was important to unite the country. Trolls are not the only characters in these tales, which often feature woodland and domestic animals that can talk and behave like humans. Foxes, bears and wolves in particular are recurrent leading characters.

The trolls depicted are often overgrown, ugly, strong and stupid with trees growing out of their noses. They live in forests and mountains and explode or are turned to stone if they catch the sun. Our perception of their appearance has been greatly influenced by the illustrator Theodor Kittelsen's many drawings of them. No other artist has brought

Norwegian folktales and trolls to life with such imagination as him. There is hardly anyone in Norway who would not recognise his drawings.

Many of the explanations provided in folktales and legends for phenomena in everyday life have their origins in the Old Norse Period and in religion. The stories may differ, but the moral of the story remains the same. Imposing mountains, deep fjords, vast forests and dark winter nights provide plenty of inspiration for supernatural phenomena.

Trolls are often closely associated with nature. They live in woodlands and deep in the mountains. At the time when folktales played a greater role in people's lives, many people lived near woods and on what nature could provide. The proximity to

nature is one of the main reasons why the belief in supernatural beings was able to survive for so long. Nature is awe-inspiring, mystical and in it lurks what many perceive to be unfathomable occurrences.

Norske folkeeventyr (Norwegian Folk Tales) by Asbjørnsen and Moe was published in 1841 and was a huge success. The stories were an important way of bringing people together and trolls became a collective term for supernatural creatures.

Illustrations by Th. Kittelsen

(From left)
Cardamom Town (at the zoo), Verdens ende (The end of the world), Vøringsfossen waterfall, the Oseberg ship.

The ten most popular attractions

The author's favourites

1. Vøringsfossen waterfall

2. Holmenkollen with the Ski Museum and ski jump

3. Tusenfryd amusement park

4. Trollstigen road, Rauma

5. Kristiansand Dyrepark zoo

6. Fløibanen funicular, Bergen

7. Hadeland Glassverk glassworks, Jevnaker

8. Festningsbyen (the Fortress Town)/Gamlebyen (the Old Town) Fredrikstad

9. Flåmsbanen railway, Aurland

10. Kjosfossen waterfall

1. Finnmarksvidda

2. Å, Lofoten

3. Fjærland and the Norwegian Glacier Museum

4. Verdens Ende [World's End], Vestfold

5. Hurtigruta, the Norwegian Coastal Voyage

6. The Viking Ship Museum, Oslo

7. Fløybanen funicular, Bergen

8. Hemsedal valley (during the winter)

9. The Norwegian Museum of Cultural History, Oslo

10. Bryggen wharf, Bergen

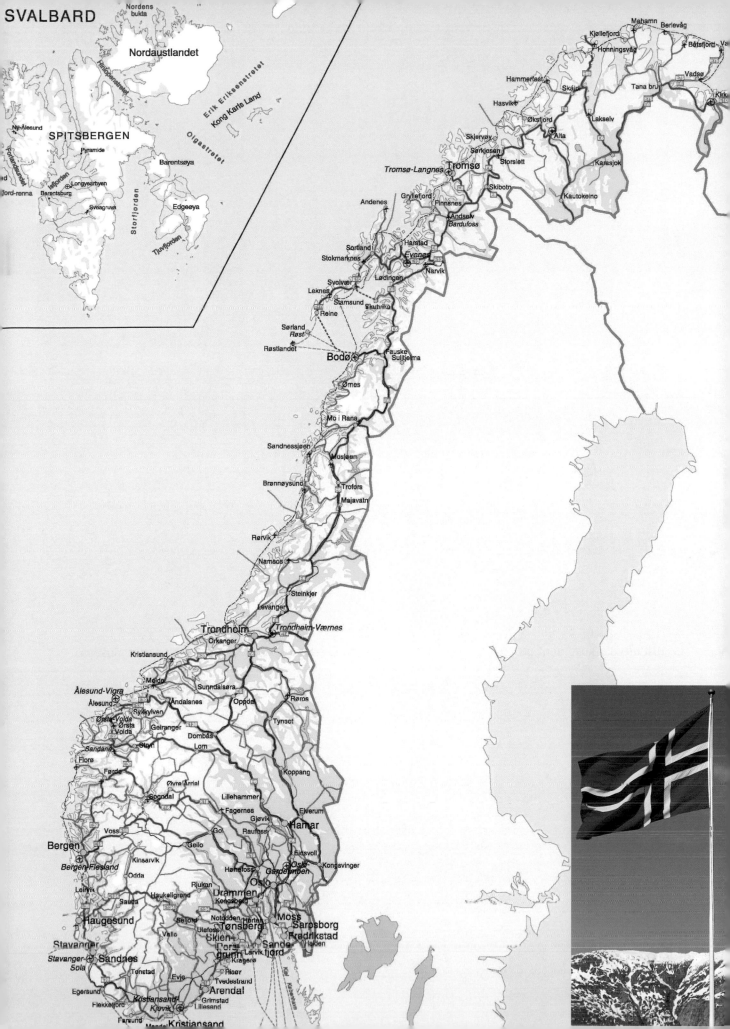

About the author

Bjørn Moholdt was born on 7 August 1959, and has travelled the length and breadth of Norway for almost a lifetime as a journalist and photographer. After lengthy and numerous trips abroad, it is nevertheless his homeland he always returns to and that fascinates him more than anything else.

Having worked as a local newspaper journalist in the country's northernmost county Finnmark, Moholdt has a thorough knowledge of the Sami culture. In his opinion, the balancing act that often arises between an ancient people and the rest of the population helps to make Norway a particularly exciting place in which to live and travel above and beyond the obviously magnificent countryside.

His many reports have been printed in a number of Norwegian newspapers and magazines. He has also contributed text and pictures to a number of books, including "The Fascinating Land I and II" (1996/1997) and "En dag i Norge" (1992).

About us

We, the Terrascope team , wish to share with you the fascination and concern for our planet. A thrill to discover and a must to preserve.
That is why we created the Terrascope series, a new way of capturing the atmosphere and impressions of your travel destinations. The books are distinctive for their stylish and easily recognisable design, lavishly endowed with photographs and the text written by local authors with knowledge and passion. This makes the Terrascope series a unique and lasting gift.
The books are available at your travel destinations. Write us a letter with comments or travel discoveries you would like to share with us. We look forward to hearing from you.

Picture credits

Top = A
Top left = B
Top right = C
Bottom = D
Bottom left = E
Bottom right = F
Centre left = G
Centre right – H
Centre = I

Arne Aasheim: 8, 59, 82, 83E, 84-85, 86, 87B, 87D, 88, 89, 90A, 90E,

Scanpix: 22

Jan Hasseleid: 69A

Nasjonalgalleriet: 106, 107

Jiri Havran: 23

Hadeland Glassverk ©: 28

KON-TIKI Museet © 27D

Neptunfoto/
Kjetil Skogli: 103A

Samfoto/
Espen Bratlie: 24, 25, 66,
Trym Ivar Bergsmo: 47, 52
Trygve Bølstad: 70
Ove Bergersen: 74-75,
Stig Tronvold: 81
Sigmund Krøvel-Velle: 93, 97A

Bård Løken: 1, 2, 3, 4-5, 6, 9, 10, 11 (11A © Vigeland-museet/BONO 2003), 12, 13, 14, 15, 16, 17, 18, 19, 20, 21, 26, 27 (27C © Geir Stormoen/BONO 2003), 29, 30, 31, 32 (32A © Kjell Nupen/BONO 2003), 33, 34, 35, 36, 37, 38-39, 40, 41, 42, 43, 44, 45, 46B, 46E, 48, 49, 50, 51, 53, 54, 55, 56-57, 58, 60, 61, 62, 63, 64, 65, 67, 68, 71, 72, 73, 76, 77, 78, 79, 80, 83A, 83F, 87C, 90F, 91, 92, 94, 95, 96, 97D, 98, 99, 100, 102, 103D, 104, 105, 108, 111, 112.
Kon Tikimuseet ©:27 D
All other photographs were taken by Bård Løken.

Statens Kartverk: 109
The boat Kagastøl in Nærøy Fjord: 112

Front cover:
Puffins
The Norwegian Flag
The Victoria on the Telemark Canal
A Sami in festive dress
Briksdalen
Fishing boats, Nykvåg
Blueberries
Bryggen wharf in Bergen
Flowers in bloom, Sørfjorden in Hardanger

Back cover:
The Northern Lights, Tromsø
The Midnight Sun, the coast of Helgeland
Boats, Geirangerfjorden
Mountain community, Tylldalen in Hedmark
Cover photos: Bård Løken